Jack and Billy and Rose

Story by Jenny Giles
Illustrations by Betty Greenhatch

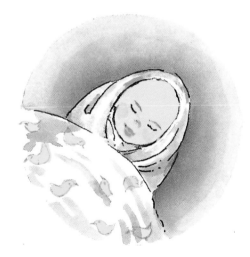

Jack went into school
with Mom and Billy.

Jack said to the teacher,
"We are getting a new baby
next week."

"A new baby!"

said the teacher.

"You are lucky.

And your new baby

will be lucky, too.

Your little baby

will have two big brothers."

On Monday, after school,
Dad and Billy came to get Jack.

"Has the baby come?" said Jack.

"No," said Billy.
"Mom is at home."

On Tuesday, after school,
Dad and Billy did not come.

Jack said to the teacher,
"All the children have gone home.
Where is my Dad?
And where is Billy?
They are very late today."

Then Jack saw Dad and Billy.

"Jack! Jack!" shouted Billy.
"The baby has come!
It's a girl.
We are going to see her now."

"Come on, boys," said Dad.
"I will take you to see Mom
and baby Rose."

"Look at baby Rose,"
said Billy.

"She is so **little**," said Jack.

"Yes," said Mom.
"Rose is your little sister.
You are my big boys, now."

"And I am a big brother like Jack," said Billy.